The Power of Small Steps

Baby Steps, Explosive
Results

A Guide to Self-Mastery

A burst of quick and powerful steps for busy people seeking transformative change. In this dynamic guide, you'll discover how tiny changes can lead to explosive results in every aspect of your life."

ONOME AKITI

ISBN:

DEDICATION

To the Creator of the Universe.

CONTENTS

Dedication   i

Acknowledgments   ii

How this book is written   iii

Foreword   iv

1   Introduction: The Power of Tiny Shifts   1

2   Understanding Habit Formation   4

3   The Habit Formula: Prompt, Routine, Reward   7

4   Cultivating Habit Attraction   10

5   Navigating Habit Satisfaction   13

6   The Art of Habit Maintenance   16

7   Overcoming Resistance: Building Resilience   19

8   Embracing Habit Evolution   22

9   The Ripple Effects of Habit Legacy   26

10   Conclusion: The Journey of Habit Transformation   28

11   The Hidden Pitfalls of   30
Good Habits

Table of Contents

Introduction: The Power of Tiny Shifts

An overview of the book's central theme: how small, incremental changes can lead to significant transformations in various aspects of life. Introduction to the concept of habit formation and its impact on personal growth and development.

Chapter 1: Understanding Habit Formation

A deep dive into the psychology of habits, exploring how habits are formed, sustained, and changed. Discussion on the Habit Loop and the role of Prompts, routines, and rewards in shaping behavior.

Chapter 2: The Habit Formula: Prompt, Routine, Reward

An exploration of the Habit Formula and its components: Prompts, routines, and rewards. Practical strategies for identifying and modifying each component to create positive habits and break negative ones.

Chapter 3: Cultivating Habit Appeal

Strategies for making desired habits more attractive and appealing, including the use of habit stacking, habit bundling, and environment design to increase habit adherence and motivation.

Chapter 4: Navigating Habit Satisfaction

Discussion on the importance of habit satisfaction and its role in maintaining long-term habit adherence. Strategies for enhancing habit satisfaction through intrinsic and extrinsic rewards.

Chapter 5: The Art of Habit Maintenance

Techniques for sustaining and reinforcing positive habits over time, including habit tracking, accountability systems, and habit rituals. Discussion on the challenges of habit maintenance and strategies for overcoming them.

Chapter 6: Overcoming Resistance: Building Resilience

Exploration of common barriers and obstacles to habit formation, including procrastination, self-doubt, and fear of failure. Strategies for building resilience and overcoming resistance to change.

Chapter 7: Embracing Habit Evolution

Discussion on the dynamic nature of habits and the importance of adapting and evolving habits to align with changing goals and circumstances. Strategies for embracing habit evolution and leveraging it for personal growth.

Chapter 8: The Ripple Effects of Habit Legacy

Exploration of how habits influence not only individual lives but also the lives of others and future generations. Stories and examples of individuals who have left a positive habit legacy and strategies for cultivating one's own.

Chapter 9: Conclusion: The Journey of Habit Transformation

Reflection on the journey of habit transformation and the key insights and principles learned throughout the book. Encouragement to continue applying these principles in daily life to achieve lasting change and fulfillment.

ACKNOWLEDGMENTS

Before we delve into the pages of "The Power of Small Steps," I would like to extend my heartfelt gratitude to those who have contributed to the realization of this book.

First and foremost, I am deeply thankful for the unwavering support and encouragement of my family. Their love, patience, and belief in my endeavors have been the cornerstone of my journey.

I am also indebted to my friends and colleagues who have provided invaluable feedback, encouragement, and inspiration throughout the writing process. Your insights have enriched this book beyond measure.

To the countless individuals whose stories of resilience and triumph have inspired the pages of this book, I offer my deepest gratitude. Your courage and perseverance serve as a beacon of hope and a testament to the transformative power of small steps.

I would like to express my appreciation to my wife and editor, whose dedication and expertise have brought this book to life. Your passion for sharing knowledge and fostering personal growth is truly commendable.

Lastly, I extend my heartfelt thanks to the readers who have chosen to embark on this journey with me. It is my sincerest hope that the insights and lessons contained within these pages will empower you to embrace the power of small steps and unlock the extraordinary potential within you.

With gratitude,

Onome Akiti

HOW THIS BOOK IS WRITTEN

Writing Style and Organization

"The Power of Small Steps" is crafted with a concise and engaging writing style, making it ideal for busy individuals seeking quick and actionable insights. Each chapter is structured to provide a burst of powerful information in a short and digestible format, ensuring that readers can easily absorb key concepts and apply them to their lives.

Short and Quick Reads:

The book is designed to cater to the needs of busy people, with each chapter offering short, focused reads that can be easily consumed during brief moments of downtime. Whether it's during a coffee break, a commute, or a spare moment between meetings, readers can dive into the book and glean valuable insights without having to commit to lengthy reading sessions.

Clear and Concise Language:

The writing is clear, concise, and accessible, avoiding unnecessary jargon or complex terminology. Concepts are explained in straightforward language, making them easy to understand and apply immediately. Each chapter delivers actionable strategies and practical tips that readers can implement right away, without getting bogged down in unnecessary detail.

Organized for Quick Reference:

The book is organized in a structured format that allows for quick reference and easy navigation. Each chapter begins with a brief introduction to the topic at hand, followed by concise explanations of key concepts and strategies. Real-life examples and anecdotes are woven throughout the text to illustrate key points and provide context for readers.

Summaries and Takeaways:

At the end of each chapter, readers will find summaries and key takeaways that distill the main points into bite-sized nuggets of wisdom. These summaries serve as handy reference points for readers to revisit later and reinforce their understanding of the material.

Actionable Insights:

Above all, "The Power of Small Steps" is focused on delivering actionable insights that readers can immediately apply to their lives. Whether it's strategies for habit formation, tips for overcoming obstacles, or techniques for fostering resilience, each chapter is packed with practical wisdom that empowers readers to take control of their habits and transform their lives one small step at a time.

Overall, "The Power of Small Steps" is designed to be a quick and impactful resource for busy individuals looking to make positive changes in their lives. With its short, quick reads and actionable insights, it's the perfect companion for anyone seeking to harness the power of habits for personal growth and transformation.

FOREWORD

Welcome to "The Power of Small Steps", a journey into the profound impact of tiny changes on our lives. As you embark on this transformative exploration, prepare to be inspired, enlightened, and empowered to unleash your fullest potential through the magic of small steps.

In a world obsessed with monumental achievements and overnight success stories, it's easy to overlook the incredible power of incremental progress. Yet, time and again, history has shown us that it's the small, consistent actions—the baby steps—that lead to the most significant transformations.

In the early 20th century, a young salesman named Joe Girard found himself struggling to make ends meet. Faced with mounting debt and dwindling prospects, Joe realized he needed a radical change if he wanted to turn his life around. But instead of seeking a grand solution, Joe took a different approach—he focused on mastering the art of customer relationships, one small interaction at a time.

Every day, Joe committed himself to sending personalized greeting cards to his clients, expressing genuine appreciation for their business. It was a simple gesture, but one that set him apart in a sea of impersonal transactions. Over time, Joe's small habit of sending cards became his signature, earning him the title of the world's greatest salesman.

By the end of his career, Joe Girard had sold more cars than anyone else in history, earning him a place in the Guinness World Records. His secret? Not flashy presentations or slick marketing tactics, but the consistent practice of a small, seemingly insignificant habit that transformed his relationships and his livelihood.

Joe Girard's story is just one of many examples scattered throughout history, illustrating the transformative power of small steps. From the artist who paints a masterpiece one brushstroke at a time to the athlete who achieves greatness through daily practice, the evidence is clear: it's the little things that add up to create something truly extraordinary.

As you delve into the pages of "The Power of Small Steps", remember Joe Girard's journey and the countless others who have harnessed the power of tiny changes to achieve remarkable results. And as you apply the principles and strategies outlined in this book to your own life, trust in the transformative potential of small steps. Embrace the journey, celebrate the progress, and watch as your life unfolds in ways you never thought possible.

Your adventure begins here. Let's take the first step together.

Warm regards,

Ishola Damilola, *B.SC, Political Science; Change Management and Life Coach, D'eliciousa International.*

Introduction: The Power of Tiny Shifts

Introduction to Small Changes

In the bustling pace of modern life, it's easy to overlook the impact of small, daily actions. We often seek dramatic transformations, not realizing that the most sustainable and profound changes come from tiny, consistent shifts. This chapter explores the concept that small changes, though seemingly insignificant, can accumulate to create significant improvements over time.

The Compound Effect

Consider the story of Emily, a graphic designer. Emily felt stuck in her career, often overwhelmed by the workload and unable to see a path forward. One day, she decided to dedicate just ten minutes each morning to learning a new design technique. At first, it seemed like a drop in the ocean. But after a year, Emily had accumulated over sixty hours of advanced skills. Her confidence soared, and she began landing more high-profile projects. This is the compound effect in action: tiny efforts compounded over time lead to remarkable results.

The Science Behind Habits

Understanding the science of habits is crucial. Our brains are wired to seek efficiency. Habits are essentially shortcuts our brains use to save effort and energy. When an action is repeated frequently, it becomes automatic, freeing up mental resources for other tasks. By harnessing this natural tendency, we can reprogram our habits to work in our favor.

The Feedback Loop

Every habit follows a feedback loop: Prompt, routine, and reward. Let's break this down:

Prompt: The trigger that initiates the behavior. It can be a specific time of day, an emotional state, or an event.
Routine: The behavior itself, the action you take in response to the Prompt.
Reward: The benefit you gain from the behavior, which reinforces the habit.

For instance, after a stressful meeting (Prompt), you might take a walk (routine) and feel relaxed (reward). Understanding this loop allows us to identify and modify our habits effectively.

Small Changes, Big Impact

Let's illustrate with another example. Meet Carlos, a marketing executive who wanted to improve his fitness. Instead of diving into a rigorous gym routine, he started with a single push-up every morning. This minuscule habit seemed almost too easy to be true, but it established a routine. Gradually, Carlos increased his push-ups, added more exercises, and eventually developed a full workout routine. By starting small, Carlos avoided the common pitfalls of burnout and unrealistic expectations.

Practical Tips for Implementing Tiny Shifts

Here are some actionable steps to integrate tiny shifts into your daily routine:

- **Identify Keystone Habits**: Focus on small changes that can trigger a positive ripple effect. For example, drinking a glass of water first thing in the morning can lead to better hydration, improved mood, and healthier eating throughout the day.

- **Use Habit Stacking**: Attach a new habit to an existing one. If you want to start meditating, do it right after brushing your teeth in the morning.

- **Track Progress:** Keep a simple log of your new habits. This visual Prompt can be highly motivating and help reinforce your commitment.

- **Be Patient:** Understand that habits take time to form. Celebrate small victories and don't be discouraged by setbacks.

The Journey Begins

Embarking on the journey of tiny shifts is empowering. It shifts the focus from grandiose plans and unattainable goals to manageable, sustainable actions. As you begin to implement these small changes, you'll start to notice a positive shift in various aspects of your life. Remember, the power lies in consistency and persistence.

In the next chapter, we will delve into the relationship between your daily habits and your overall identity, exploring how the smallest actions can redefine who you are. Stay tuned and get ready to discover the profound impact of incremental change.

CHAPTER 1: UNDERSTANDING HABIT FORMATION

The Identity-Action Loop

Every action we take is a vote for the type of person we wish to become. The concept of identity is deeply intertwined with our habits. When we consistently perform actions that align with our desired identity, we start to embody that identity. This chapter explores how our daily habits shape our identity and how we can use this understanding to transform ourselves.

Who Do You Want to Be?

Think about Maria, an aspiring writer. She had always dreamed of writing a novel, but she struggled with self-doubt and procrastination. Maria decided to start small by writing for ten minutes every morning. Initially, it wasn't about producing a bestseller but about proving to herself that she was a writer. Over time, these small writing sessions accumulated, and Maria began to see herself as a writer. Her new identity fueled her motivation, and she eventually completed her first manuscript.

The Power of Self-Perception

Our actions reinforce our self-perception. If you view yourself as someone who is active and healthy, you're more likely to engage in behaviors that support that identity, such as exercising regularly and eating nutritious foods. Conversely, if you see yourself as someone who struggles with organization, you're more likely to perpetuate disorganized behaviors. The key is to align your habits with the identity you aspire to achieve.

The Identity Transformation Framework

To transform your identity through habits, follow these steps:

1. **Define Your Desired Identity:**
   Clearly articulate the person you want to become. This could be a specific role (e.g., a runner, a painter) or a general trait (e.g., organized, mindful).

2. **Identify Habits That Align with This Identity:**
   List small, manageable habits that align with your desired identity. If you want to become a more mindful person, you might start with a five-minute daily meditation.

3. **Start Small and Be Consistent:**
   Begin with tiny habits that are easy to maintain. The goal is to create a pattern of behavior that reinforces your desired identity.

4. **Reinforce Your Identity with Each Action:**
   Every time you perform your habit, consciously acknowledge that you are reinforcing your desired identity. This reinforcement strengthens your self-perception and commitment.

The Story of John: From Couch Potato to Runner

John had always considered himself a couch potato. He admired marathon runners but felt that lifestyle was out of reach. One day, he decided to redefine his identity. He started with a simple habit: walking for five minutes each day. As this became routine, he gradually increased the duration and intensity. Each small action was a vote for his new identity as an active person. Over time, John's identity shifted from couch potato to runner, and he eventually completed his first marathon.

Real-Life Example: *Michael Phelps and the Power of Routine*

Michael Phelps, the most decorated Olympian of all time, owes much of his success to the power of routine and the meticulous formation of habits. From a young age, Phelps's coach, Bob Bowman, emphasized the importance of consistent and structured habits both in and out of the pool.

One of the most notable aspects of Phelps's routine was his pre-race ritual. Before every race, Phelps followed the same series of actions: he would wake up at the same time, eat the same breakfast (usually consisting of a large number of calories to fuel his intense training), and arrive at the pool to begin his warm-up. He would listen to the same music playlist on his headphones, which helped him get into the right mental state.

A particularly powerful example of Phelps's habit formation was the visualization technique instilled in him by Bowman. Every night before going to sleep, Phelps would visualize himself swimming a perfect race. He would imagine every stroke, every turn, and every detail of his performance. This mental rehearsal was so detailed that he could feel the water on his skin and hear the sounds of the pool.

One of the most dramatic demonstrations of the power of these habits came during the 2008 Beijing Olympics. In the 200-meter butterfly final, Phelps's goggles began to leak water, eventually filling up completely. For many athletes, this would have been a disaster. However, Phelps remained calm. Because of his extensive visualization practice, he had mentally rehearsed how to swim blind. He relied on his muscle memory and his pre-race habits to count his strokes and make the turns.

Phelps completed the race and won the gold medal, setting a new world record despite not being able to see for most of the race. His ability to stay calm and rely on his ingrained habits allowed him to perform under pressure and overcome a significant challenge.

Michael Phelps's story illustrates the profound impact that well-formed habits can have on performance. By understanding and developing these habits through consistent practice and mental preparation, Phelps was able to achieve extraordinary success and become a legendary athlete.[1]

This real-life story of Michael Phelps demonstrates the importance of understanding and forming effective habits, highlighting how structured routines and mental preparation can lead to exceptional achievements.

Practical Tips for Identity-Based Habits

1. Visualize Your Desired Identity:

---

[1]Reference: Phelps, M., & Abrahamson, A. (2009). No Limits: The Will to Succeed. Simon & Schuster.

Spend a few minutes each day visualizing yourself embodying your desired identity. This mental practice can reinforce your commitment and motivation.

2. **Use Affirmations:**
    Create positive affirmations that reflect your desired identity. Repeat them daily to reinforce your new self-perception.

3. **Seek Role Models:**
    Identify role models who embody the identity you aspire to. Learn from their habits and behaviors, and let their success inspire you.

4. **Reflect on Your Progress:**
    Regularly reflect on your actions and how they align with your desired identity. Celebrate small victories and acknowledge your growth.

Embracing the Journey

Transforming your identity through habits is a journey, not a destination. It's about continuously evolving and aligning your actions with the person you want to become. As you integrate identity-based habits into your life, you'll notice a profound shift in your self-perception and overall satisfaction.

In the next chapter, we will explore the foundational principles of behavior change, providing a deeper understanding of how to effectively build and sustain new habits. Stay committed to your journey, and remember that every small action is a step towards becoming the best version of yourself.

Chapter 2: Unveiling the Habit Formula

Introduction to Behavior Change

Change is a constant in life, yet many struggle to implement lasting transformations. This chapter introduces the Habit Formula, a powerful framework that demystifies the process of behavior change. By understanding the underlying principles, you can effectively build new habits and break old ones.

The Habit Formula Unveiled

The Habit Formula consists of four fundamental laws:

Clarity of Prompt: *Make it Overt (noticeable).*
Attraction of Routine: *Make it appealing.*
Ease of Action: *Make it simple.*
Satisfaction of Reward: *Make it enjoyable.*

Law 1: Make It Overt

The first step in habit formation is to make the Prompt overt (obvious, noticaceble). This can be achieved by:

- **Environment Design**: Arrange your environment to visually Prompt the desired behavior. For example, place a bowl of fruit on the kitchen counter to encourage healthier snacking.
- **Implementation Intentions**: Specify when and where you will perform the habit. This increases the likelihood of follow-through.

Law 2: Make It Appealing

The more appealing a habit is, the more likely you are to stick with it. Strategies to make habits appealing include:

- **Temptation Bundling**: Pair an enjoyable activity with a habit you want to adopt. For instance, only allowing yourself to watch your favorite TV show while exercising.
- **Habit Stacking**: Attach the new habit to an existing routine. This capitalizes on the momentum of established behaviors.

Law 3: Make It Simple

Habits should be easy to perform to minimize resistance. Ways to make habits simple include:

- **Two-Minute Rule**: Start with a habit that takes less than two minutes to do. Once you've started, it's easier to keep going.
- **Environment Optimization**: Remove friction and barriers that hinder habit formation. For example, lay out workout clothes the night before to streamline the morning routine.

Law 4: Make It Enjoyable

Rewards reinforce habits and increase the likelihood of repetition. To make habits enjoyable:

- **Immediate Rewards**: Link immediate gratification to habit completion. Celebrate small wins to create positive associations with the behavior.
- **Track Progress**: Use visual Prompts and habit trackers to monitor your progress. Seeing your improvement over time can be highly motivating.

The Habit Formula in Action: Sarah's Story

Sarah struggled to establish a consistent exercise routine until she applied the Habit Formula. She made her workout clothes visible (obvious), scheduled workouts with a friend (attractive), started with short, easy sessions (easy), and rewarded herself with a relaxing bath afterward (satisfying). By aligning her habits with the Habit Formula, Sarah transformed her fitness habits and achieved her goals.

Real-Life Example: *Starbucks and the Customer Service Transformation*

Starbucks, the global coffeehouse chain, is renowned for its customer service. But in the early 2000s, the company faced a challenge: maintaining high levels of customer service as it rapidly expanded. The solution lay in understanding and implementing the habit formula of prompt, routine, and reward.

Howard Behar, then-president of Starbucks, recognized that the company needed to create consistent service habits among its baristas. To achieve this, Starbucks developed a comprehensive training program focused on the habit loop: prompt, routine, and reward.

Prompt: The prompt for Starbucks baristas is a customer's order. This is the trigger that initiates the routine.

Routine: Starbucks created specific routines for its baristas to follow in response to this prompt. The routines included not just the technical aspects of making coffee but also interpersonal skills. Baristas were trained to engage with customers, make eye contact, and create a welcoming environment. One key routine was the LATTE method: Listen, Acknowledge, Take action, Thank, and Explain. This method ensured that baristas had a clear and repeatable process for handling customer complaints and ensuring customer satisfaction.

Reward: The reward for the baristas was multifaceted. On one level, there was immediate gratification from a customer's smile or a simple thank you. On another level, Starbucks implemented a system of recognition and rewards for exceptional service, including positive feedback from managers and opportunities for career advancement within the company.

One illustrative story involves a Starbucks barista named Brad. Brad worked at a busy downtown location and often dealt with frustrated and hurried customers. By consistently applying the LATTE method, Brad transformed many potentially negative interactions into positive experiences. For example, when a regular customer, Mr. Johnson, was upset about his incorrect order, Brad used the LATTE method to defuse the situation. He listened to Mr. Johnson's complaint, acknowledged the mistake, took immediate action to correct the order, thanked him for his patience, and explained the steps taken to prevent future mistakes. This approach not only resolved the issue but turned Mr. Johnson into a loyal customer.

Through the consistent application of the habit loop, Starbucks was able to create a reliable and high-quality customer experience across its stores. Baristas like Brad exemplified how the habit formula of prompt, routine, and reward could transform service and build lasting customer relationships.

This systematic approach to customer service helped Starbucks differentiate itself in a crowded market and foster a strong brand reputation. The success of this habit-based training program demonstrates the power of understanding and applying the habit formula in a business context.[2]

This real-life story of Starbucks highlights how understanding and implementing the habit formula can lead to significant improvements in performance and customer satisfaction, showcasing the transformative power of structured habits in a corporate environment.

Practical Application of the Habit Formula

- **Audit Your Environment**: Identify Prompts and triggers that prompt both desired and undesired behaviors. Modify your surroundings to support positive habits.
- **Optimize Your Routine**: Make habits appealing and effortless by integrating them into existing routines and adding attractive elements.
- **Maximize Rewards**: Design immediate rewards and track your progress to reinforce habits and maintain motivation.

Conclusion: Harnessing the Power of the Habit Formula

By applying the Habit Formula, you can unlock the potential for lasting behavior change. Remember, habits are not formed overnight; they require consistent effort and commitment. Embrace the Habit Formula as your guide and watch as small changes compound into significant transformations.

In the next chapter, we will delve deeper into the concept of making habits attractive, exploring strategies to leverage human psychology in habit formation. Get ready to uncover the secrets of irresistible habits.

---

[2] Reference: Duhigg, C. (2012). The Power of Habit: Why We Do What We Do in Life and Business. Random House.

Chapter 3: The Art of Habit Appeal

Introduction: The Magnetic Pull of Habits
Habits have a gravitational pull, drawing us toward certain behaviors, both positive and negative. In this chapter, we explore the art of habit appeal—how to make desirable habits irresistible and repel those that hinder our progress. By understanding the psychology behind habit attraction, you can design environments that naturally lead to positive behaviors.

The Psychology of Appeal
Appeal or attraction is not just about physical allure; it's deeply rooted in psychology. Understanding the psychological drivers of behavior can help us create environments that cultivate desirable habits. Some key psychological principles include:

- **Instant Gratification**: Humans are wired to seek immediate rewards. By providing instant gratification for desirable habits, we increase their attractiveness.
- **Social Proof**: We tend to mimic the behavior of others, especially those we admire or identify with. Leveraging social proof can make habits more appealing.
- **Scarcity**: The perception of scarcity increases the value of a behavior. Creating a sense of scarcity around desirable habits can enhance their allure.

Leveraging Instant Gratification
Instant gratification is a powerful motivator for behavior. To make habits more attractive:

- **Immediate Rewards**: Offer immediate rewards for completing desired behaviors. This can be as simple as a tasty snack after a workout or a few minutes of relaxation after completing a task.
- **Gamification**: Turn habits into games with clear rules and rewards. Tracking progress and earning points can make habits feel more rewarding and enjoyable.

Harnessing Social Influence

Humans are inherently social creatures, and we often look to others for Prompts on how to behave. To leverage social influence in habit formation:

- **Accountability Partners**: Pair up with a friend or partner to hold each other accountable for habit adherence. The social pressure can motivate both parties to stick to their commitments.
- **Joining Communities**: Participate in groups or communities that share your goals and values. Surrounding yourself with like-minded individuals can provide support, encouragement, and inspiration.

Creating a Sense of Scarcity

Scarcity enhances the perceived value of a behavior, making it more attractive. Strategies to create scarcity around habits include:

- **Limited-Time Offers**: Set time-bound challenges or goals to create a sense of urgency. For example, committing to a 30-day fitness challenge can make exercise feel more compelling.
- **Exclusive Access**: Offer exclusive content or benefits to those who engage in desired behaviors. This can incentivize participation and increase the perceived value of the habit.

The Story of Mark: Cultivating a Habit of Gratitude

Mark struggled with negativity and wanted to cultivate a habit of gratitude. He implemented the Habit Appeal techniques by keeping a gratitude journal (immediate reward), sharing his entries with a supportive online community (social influence), and setting a daily gratitude challenge for himself (scarcity). Over time, gratitude became an ingrained habit, transforming Mark's outlook on life.

Real-Life Example: *Peloton and the Personalized Fitness Experience*

Peloton, the innovative fitness company, has revolutionized the way people exercise by tapping into the power of habit appeal. At the heart of Peloton's success is its ability to make exercise not only effective but also enjoyable and addictive through personalized experiences.

Creating the Prompt:

Peloton's interactive exercise equipment, such as its stationary bikes and treadmills, serve as powerful prompts for users to engage in physical activity. With sleek design and easy accessibility, these devices beckon users to begin their workout routines with just a touch of a button.

Crafting the Routine:

Peloton offers a wide range of workout classes, from cycling and running to strength training and yoga, each led by charismatic and motivational instructors. These classes are carefully curated to cater to various fitness levels, preferences, and goals, ensuring that users find routines that resonate with them. By providing diverse and engaging content, Peloton encourages users to establish regular workout habits that they genuinely enjoy.

Delivering the Reward:

Peloton excels in delivering rewarding experiences to its users. Beyond the physical benefits of exercise, Peloton offers a sense of community and accomplishment. Users can track their progress, compete with friends and fellow Peloton members, and celebrate milestones together. Additionally, Peloton's subscription model provides access to a vast library of on-demand classes, allowing users to discover new workouts and instructors, keeping their routines fresh and exciting.

An illustrative example is Sarah, a Peloton user who struggled to stay motivated with her fitness routine. After purchasing a Peloton bike, Sarah found herself eagerly anticipating her daily workouts. The combination of immersive classes, supportive community, and tangible progress tracking kept her engaged and committed to her fitness goals. Over time, exercise transformed from a chore to a cherished habit that brought her joy and fulfillment.

By understanding the art of habit appeal, Peloton has succeeded in creating a fitness ecosystem that transcends traditional exercise paradigms. Its emphasis on personalized experiences, community engagement, and intrinsic rewards has fostered a loyal user base and positioned Peloton as a leader in the fitness industry.

Peloton's story serves as a compelling example of how businesses can leverage habit appeal to not only attract customers but also foster long-term engagement and loyalty.[3]

This real-life story of Peloton demonstrates how the art of habit appeal can transform mundane activities like exercise into enjoyable and addictive routines, showcasing the potential for businesses to create compelling experiences that resonate with users on a deeper level.

Practical Application of Habit Appeal Techniques

- **Identify Key Rewards**: Determine what immediate rewards would make your desired habits more attractive.
- **Build a Support Network**: Surround yourself with individuals who support and encourage your habit formation journey.
- **Create Scarcity**: Introduce elements of scarcity to increase the perceived value of your habits and behaviors.

Conclusion: Embracing the Power of Appeal and Attraction

By harnessing the principles of habit appeal (attraction), you can create environments that naturally draw you toward positive behaviors. Whether it's through instant gratification, social influence, or scarcity, the art of habit appeal empowers you to design a lifestyle aligned with your goals and values.

In the next chapter, we will explore the concept of habit simplicity—how to streamline habits for maximum effectiveness and efficiency. Get ready to simplify your habits and amplify your results.

---

[3] Reference: Peloton Website and User Testimonials.

Chapter 4: Streamlining Habits for Success

Introduction: The Beauty of Habit Simplicity
In a world filled with complexity, simplicity is a breath of fresh air. This chapter explores the art of habit simplicity—how to streamline your habits for maximum effectiveness and efficiency. By decluttering your routines and focusing on essential actions, you can amplify your results and minimize decision fatigue.

The Principle of Minimalism
Minimalism is more than just an aesthetic; it's a way of life. At its core, minimalism is about focusing on what truly matters and eliminating distractions. Applying minimalism to your habits involves:

- **Identifying Essential Behaviors**: Determine the core actions that will move you closer to your goals.
- **Eliminating Non-Essentials**: Cut out unnecessary tasks and commitments that drain your time and energy.

The Two-Minute Rule
The Two-Minute Rule is a powerful tool for habit simplicity. It states that if a habit takes less than two minutes to complete, you should do it immediately. This rule capitalizes on the principle of momentum—once you've started a task, it's easier to keep going. By breaking habits down into small, manageable chunks, you remove barriers to entry and increase the likelihood of follow-through.

Habit Stacking Revisited

Habit stacking is another strategy for simplifying habits. By attaching new behaviors to existing routines, you can piggyback on established habits and streamline your daily rituals. To effectively stack habits:

- **Identify Anchor Habits**: Choose existing routines that serve as natural Prompts for new behaviors.
- **Pair Habits Thoughtfully:** Ensure that the new habit complements the anchor habit and flows seamlessly into your routine.

The Power of Routine

Routines provide structure and stability in an otherwise chaotic world. By establishing daily rituals, you can automate mundane tasks and free up mental bandwidth for more important endeavors. To create an effective routine:

- **Prioritize Your Day**: Identify the most important tasks and allocate time for them in your schedule.
- **Batch Similar Activities**: Group similar tasks together to minimize context switching and maximize efficiency.

The Story of Emma: Simplifying Her Morning Routine

Emma struggled with overwhelm every morning as she juggled multiple tasks before heading to work. She decided to simplify her routine by implementing the Two-Minute Rule and habit stacking. She started by making her bed (Two-Minute Rule), followed by a brief meditation session (habit stacking with brushing teeth). These small changes transformed her mornings, reducing stress and increasing productivity.

Real-Life Example: *Warren Buffett and the Power of Focus*

Warren Buffett, one of the most successful investors of all time, is renowned not just for his financial acumen but also for his ability to focus intensely on his goals. Buffett's streamlined approach to habits and decision-making has been a key factor in his success.

Early in his career, Buffett developed a habit of rigorous and focused reading. He would spend hours each day reading annual reports, financial statements, and a wide range of books and articles on various industries. This habit allowed him to accumulate a vast amount of knowledge, which he could then apply to his investment decisions.

Buffett's streamlined habits are evident in his famous "20-Slot Rule." He advises that one should act as if they have a punch card with only 20 slots for investments over their lifetime. This metaphor encourages making fewer but more carefully considered decisions, focusing on high-quality opportunities. By concentrating on fewer investments, Buffett could devote more time and energy to understanding each one deeply, leading to better outcomes.

Another example of Buffett's streamlined habits is his daily routine. He keeps his schedule remarkably free of unnecessary meetings and commitments, allowing him to focus on his most important tasks. Buffett famously starts his day by reading newspapers and financial reports, ensuring he stays well-informed and can make timely decisions.

Buffett's partnership with Charlie Munger also exemplifies streamlined habits. Both investors share a commitment to continuous learning and rigorous analysis, often discussing ideas for hours to refine their thinking. This habit of disciplined dialogue and reflection has helped them avoid many investment pitfalls and capitalize on high-quality opportunities.

By focusing on a few key habits—intensive reading, deliberate decision-making, and maintaining a clear schedule—Buffett has achieved extraordinary success. His story illustrates how streamlining habits can lead to more effective use of time and resources, ultimately driving remarkable achievements.[4]

This real-life story of Warren Buffett underscores the importance of streamlining habits to focus on what truly matters, providing a powerful example for readers seeking to achieve success through effective habit management.

Practical Tips for Habit Simplicity

Start Small: Break habits down into bite-sized actions that take no more than two minutes to complete.

- **Harness Existing Routines**: Piggyback on established habits to streamline your new behaviors.

---

[4] Reference: Schroeder, A. (2008). The Snowball: Warren Buffett and the Business of Life. Bantam Books.

- **Create Daily Rituals**: Establish consistent routines that provide structure and efficiency to your day.

Conclusion: Embracing the Power of Simplicity

In a world filled with noise and distractions, simplicity is a beacon of clarity. By streamlining your habits and focusing on essential actions, you can amplify your results and achieve greater success with less effort. Embrace the beauty of habit simplicity and watch as your life transforms before your eyes.

In the next chapter, we will explore the concept of habit satisfaction—how to cultivate a sense of fulfillment and reward from your daily behaviors. Get ready to elevate your habits to new heights of satisfaction.

CHAPTER 5: CULTIVATING HABIT SATISFACTION

Introduction: The Missing Piece of the Habit Puzzle

Habits are more than just robotic actions; they're pathways to fulfillment and satisfaction. In this chapter, we explore the importance of habit satisfaction—how to cultivate a sense of joy and reward from your daily behaviors. By infusing your habits with meaning and pleasure, you can enhance your overall well-being and motivation.

The Role of Dopamine

Dopamine is often referred to as the "feel-good" neurotransmitter—it plays a central role in our brain's reward system. When we engage in pleasurable activities, our brains release dopamine, reinforcing the associated behaviors. By understanding how dopamine influences habit formation, we can leverage its power to create more satisfying habits.

The Habit Satisfaction Framework

The Habit Satisfaction Framework consists of three components:

- **Intrinsic Rewards**: Internal sources of satisfaction derived directly from the behavior itself.
- **Extrinsic Rewards**: External incentives or reinforcements that enhance the enjoyment of the behavior.
- **Meaningful Connections:** The deeper purpose or significance behind the habit, which adds a layer of fulfillment beyond immediate rewards.

Cultivating Intrinsic Rewards

Intrinsic rewards are the most sustainable source of habit satisfaction because they come from within. Strategies to cultivate intrinsic rewards include:

- **Mindful Presence**: Fully immerse yourself in the present moment during habit execution, savoring each sensation and experience.
- **Embracing Progress**: Celebrate small victories and milestones along your habit journey, acknowledging your growth and improvement.
- **Finding Flow**: Seek activities that challenge and engage you at the perfect balance of skill and difficulty, leading to a state of flow where time seems to stand still.

Enhancing Extrinsic Rewards

Extrinsic rewards can amplify habit satisfaction by providing additional incentives and reinforcements. Ways to enhance extrinsic rewards include:

- **Reward Systems**: Implement tangible rewards for habit completion, such as a treat or a small indulgence.
- **Social Reinforcement**: Share your progress and accomplishments with others, receiving validation and support from your social circle.
- **Gamification**: Turn habits into a game with clear goals, rules, and rewards, making them more engaging and enjoyable.

Discovering Meaningful Connections

Meaningful connections infuse habits with purpose and significance, elevating them beyond mere tasks. To discover meaningful connections:

- **Clarify Your Values**: Reflect on what truly matters to you and how your habits align with your core values.
- **Set Meaningful Goals**: Establish goals that resonate with your values and aspirations, providing a sense of direction and purpose.
- **Contribute to Something Bigger:** Engage in habits that serve a greater cause or benefit others, fostering a sense of fulfillment and impact.

The Story of Alex: Finding Joy in Daily Exercise

Alex struggled to maintain a consistent exercise routine until he discovered the power of habit satisfaction. He shifted his focus from external goals (like weight loss) to intrinsic rewards (like the feeling of strength and vitality). By embracing the joy of movement and the sense of accomplishment from each workout, exercise became a source of pleasure rather than a chore.

Real-Life Example: *Duolingo and the Joy of Language Learning*
Duolingo, the popular language-learning app, has mastered the art of cultivating habit satisfaction by making language learning not only effective but also enjoyable and rewarding.

Creating the Prompt:

Duolingo's user-friendly interface and gamified approach serve as powerful Prompts for users to engage in language learning. The app's vibrant design, cheerful mascot, and daily notifications prompt users to begin their language lessons, signaling the start of a rewarding journey.

Crafting the Routine:

Duolingo offers bite-sized lessons that cater to different proficiency levels and learning styles. Users can choose from a variety of languages and topics, allowing them to personalize their learning experience. The app employs spaced repetition algorithms and interactive exercises to keep users engaged and motivated throughout their language-learning journey.

Delivering the Reward:

Duolingo excels in delivering immediate and tangible rewards to its users. Each lesson completed earns users experience points (XP), which contribute to their overall progress and unlock achievements. Additionally, Duolingo employs a system of streaks and daily goals to encourage consistency and habit formation. Users also have the option to compete with friends or join language clubs, fostering a sense of community and friendly competition.

An illustrative example is Maria, a Duolingo user who always dreamed of learning French but struggled to find the time and motivation to do so. After discovering Duolingo, Maria found herself captivated by the app's interactive lessons and engaging challenges. The sense of accomplishment she felt after completing each lesson motivated her to continue her language-learning journey. Over time, Maria's proficiency in French improved significantly, and she even connected with other learners through Duolingo's community features.

By prioritizing user satisfaction and engagement, Duolingo has become a leading platform for language learning, with millions of users worldwide. Its emphasis on gamification, personalization, and immediate rewards has transformed language learning from a daunting task into an enjoyable and rewarding habit.

Duolingo's story serves as a compelling example of how businesses can cultivate habit satisfaction by delivering meaningful and rewarding experiences to their users, ultimately fostering long-term engagement and loyalty.[5]

This real-life story of Duolingo demonstrates how cultivating habit satisfaction can turn seemingly challenging tasks, like language learning, into enjoyable and rewarding experiences, showcasing the potential for businesses to create compelling products that resonate with users and drive long-term engagement.

Practical Tips for Habit Satisfaction

- **Engage Mindfully**: Be fully present during habit execution, savoring each moment and sensation.
- **Reward Yourself**: Implement tangible rewards for habit completion to enhance motivation and enjoyment.
- **Align with Values**: Ensure your habits align with your core values and aspirations, providing a sense of purpose and fulfillment.

Conclusion: Embracing the Joy of Habit Satisfaction

Habits are not just a means to an end; they are opportunities for growth, joy, and fulfillment. By infusing your habits with meaning, pleasure, and reward, you can create a life rich in satisfaction and purpose. Embrace the Habit Satisfaction Framework as your guide and watch as your daily behaviors become sources of profound fulfillment.

---

[5] Reference: Duolingo Website and User Testimonials

Chapter 6: Mastering Habit Maintenance

Introduction: The Journey of Habit Mastery

Building habits is just the beginning; maintaining them over the long term is where true mastery lies. In this chapter, we explore the art of habit maintenance—how to sustain your habits despite challenges and setbacks. By adopting strategies for resilience and perseverance, you can ensure lasting success on your habit journey.

The Habit Maintenance Mindset

Maintaining habits requires a shift in mindset from short-term focus to long-term sustainability. Cultivating a habit maintenance mindset involves:

- **Embracing Imperfection**: Accept that setbacks and slip-ups are natural parts of the habit journey. Instead of dwelling on failures, focus on learning and growth.
- **Prioritizing Consistency**: Consistency is key to habit maintenance. Make your habits non-negotiable by integrating them into your daily routine.
- **Cultivating Resilience**: Develop resilience to overcome obstacles and setbacks. See challenges as opportunities for growth rather than reasons to give up.

Overcoming Common Challenges

Habit maintenance is not without its challenges. Some common obstacles and strategies for overcoming them include:

- **Lack of Motivation**: Reconnect with your why and remind yourself of the benefits of your habits. Break tasks into smaller, more manageable steps to reduce overwhelm.

- **Time Constraints:** Prioritize your habits by scheduling them into your day and eliminating non-essential tasks. Look for pockets of time throughout your day to fit in habit activities.
- **Plateaus and Plateauing:** Plateaus are a natural part of the habit journey. Stay patient and trust the process. Experiment with new approaches and strategies to break through plateaus and reignite progress.

The Power of Habit Streaks

Habit streaks can be powerful motivators for maintaining consistency. By tracking your consecutive days of habit adherence, you create a visual representation of your progress and commitment. Strategies for maintaining habit streaks include:

- **Start Small:** Begin with manageable habits to build momentum and confidence. As your streak grows, gradually increase the challenge.
- **Stay Accountable**: Share your habit streaks with a friend or accountability partner for added motivation and support.
- **Celebrate Milestones:** Celebrate milestones along your streak journey, whether it's reaching a certain number of days or achieving a personal best.

The Story of Lily: Navigating the Ups and Downs of Habit Maintenance

Lily embarked on a habit journey to improve her productivity and well-being. Along the way, she encountered challenges, including busy periods at work and periods of low motivation. Through resilience and perseverance, she learned to adapt her habits to fit her changing circumstances, maintaining consistency despite setbacks. Over time, habit maintenance became second nature, leading to a lasting transformation in Lily's life.

Real-Life Example: *Fitbit and the Journey to Health*

Fitbit, the wearable fitness technology company, has revolutionized the way people track and maintain their health habits through its innovative devices and ecosystem.

Creating the Prompt:

Fitbit's wearable devices, such as fitness trackers and smartwatches, serve as constant reminders and Prompts for users to prioritize their health and fitness goals. The devices track various metrics, including steps taken, distance traveled, calories burned, and sleep patterns, providing users with real-time feedback on their daily activities.

Crafting the Routine:

Fitbit offers a comprehensive ecosystem of health and fitness features and services to help users establish and maintain healthy habits. The Fitbit app provides personalized insights, goal setting, and challenges to keep users motivated and engaged. Users can also access a library of guided workouts, meditation sessions, and nutrition tracking tools to support their overall well-being.

Delivering the Reward:

Fitbit excels in delivering tangible rewards and incentives to its users. Achieving daily step goals, hitting personal records, and completing challenges earn users badges and rewards, fostering a sense of accomplishment and progress. Fitbit's social features allow users to connect with friends, family, and fellow Fitbit users, providing support, accountability, and friendly competition.

An illustrative example is John, a Fitbit user who struggled with maintaining an active lifestyle due to his sedentary job and busy schedule. After purchasing a Fitbit device, John became more aware of his daily activity levels and gradually incorporated more movement into his routine. Setting and achieving daily step goals motivated John to take the stairs instead of the elevator, go for walks during his lunch break, and participate in weekend hikes with friends. Over time, John's consistency and commitment to his health habits led to significant improvements in his fitness and overall well-being.

By empowering users with tools, insights, and rewards, Fitbit has helped millions of people worldwide master the maintenance of their health habits. Its user-centric approach to habit maintenance has made it a trusted companion on the journey to better health and fitness.

Fitbit's story serves as a compelling example of how businesses can support habit maintenance by providing users with the tools, motivation, and community they need to stay on track and achieve their goals.[6]

This real-life story of Fitbit demonstrates how mastering habit maintenance can lead to significant improvements in health and well-being, showcasing the potential for businesses to create products and services that empower users to sustain positive habits and achieve their goals.

Practical Tips for Habit Maintenance

- **Stay Consistent:** Make your habits non-negotiable by integrating them into your daily routine.
- **Cultivate Resilience**: Develop resilience to overcome obstacles and setbacks on your habit journey.
- **Track Your Progress**: Use habit streaks to visually track your consistency and stay motivated.

Conclusion: Becoming a Master of Habit Maintenance

Habit maintenance is the cornerstone of lasting behavior change. By adopting a habit maintenance mindset, overcoming common challenges, and leveraging the power of habit streaks, you can become a master of habit maintenance. Embrace the journey of continuous improvement and watch as your habits transform your life.

---

[6] Reference: Fitbit Website and User Testimonials

CHAPTER 7: EMBRACING HABIT EVOLUTION

Introduction: The Fluid Nature of Habit Formation

Habits are not static; they evolve and adapt over time as we grow and change. In this chapter, we explore the concept of habit evolution—how to adapt and refine your habits to align with your evolving goals and values. By embracing the fluidity of habit formation, you can ensure that your habits continue to serve you well throughout your journey.

Understanding Habit Dynamics

Habits are influenced by various factors, including:

- **Life Transitions:** Changes in circumstances, such as starting a new job or moving to a new city, can disrupt existing habits and create opportunities for new ones.
- **Personal Growth:** As we grow and evolve, our priorities and values may shift, leading to changes in our habits to reflect our evolving aspirations.
- **External Influences:** External factors, such as societal trends or technological advancements, can impact the habits we form and the behaviors we engage in.

The Process of Habit Evolution

Habit evolution involves a deliberate process of reflection, adaptation, and refinement:

- **Reflection:** Take time to reflect on your current habits and assess whether they are still serving your goals and values.

- **Adaptation**: Identify areas where your habits could be improved or aligned more closely with your current priorities.
- **Refinement**: Experiment with new habits and approaches, refining your routines to better support your evolving aspirations.

Navigating Life Transitions

Life transitions provide opportunities for habit evolution. Strategies for navigating transitions include:

1. **Embrace Flexibility**: Be willing to adapt your habits to fit your changing circumstances.
- **Set Realistic Expectations**: Recognize that transitions may disrupt your routines temporarily. Be patient with yourself as you adjust.
- **Focus on Core Habits:** Prioritize essential habits that provide stability and support during times of change.

Embracing Personal Growth

Personal growth often involves shedding old habits and adopting new ones that better align with our evolving values and aspirations. Strategies for embracing personal growth include:

1. **Set Intentions**: Clarify your intentions and values to guide your habit evolution journey.
- **Experiment with New Habits**: Be open to trying new things and experimenting with different approaches to see what resonates with you.
- **Celebrate Progress**: Celebrate the progress you've made on your habit journey, recognizing the growth and transformation you've experienced along the way.

The Story of David: Embracing Habit Evolution in Retirement

David faced a significant life transition when he retired from his long-time career. He took the opportunity to reflect on his habits and priorities, realizing that some no longer served him in this new phase of life. David embraced habit evolution by experimenting with new hobbies and routines, eventually finding fulfillment in activities he had never considered before retirement.

Real-Life Example: *Netflix and the Evolution of Viewing Habits*

Netflix, the global streaming giant, has embraced habit evolution by continuously adapting its platform and content offerings to meet the changing preferences and behaviors of its users.

Recognizing the Need for Change:

In the early days of Netflix, the company revolutionized the way people watched movies and TV shows by offering a convenient and affordable alternative to traditional cable and DVD rentals. However, as technology and consumer preferences evolved, Netflix recognized the need to adapt its business model to remain competitive in an increasingly crowded market.

Embracing Innovation:

Netflix embraced innovation by investing heavily in original content production and developing sophisticated recommendation algorithms to personalize the viewing experience for each user. By analyzing viewing habits and preferences, Netflix could recommend relevant titles and curate customized content categories, such as "Trending Now" and "Because You Watched," to keep users engaged and entertained.

Adapting to New Trends:

As streaming habits shifted towards binge-watching and on-demand viewing, Netflix responded by releasing entire seasons of original series at once, allowing users to consume content at their own pace. This shift in release strategy not only catered to changing viewing habits but also created a sense of anticipation and excitement among subscribers.

Staying Ahead of the Curve:

Netflix continues to stay ahead of the curve by experimenting with new formats, genres, and interactive features to enhance the user experience. From interactive storytelling in shows like "Black Mirror: Bandersnatch" to innovative content partnerships with renowned filmmakers and creators, Netflix remains at the forefront of entertainment innovation.

An illustrative example is Jane, a long-time Netflix subscriber who initially joined the platform to watch popular TV shows and movies. Over time, Jane's viewing habits evolved as she discovered and explored new genres and original series recommended by Netflix's algorithms. Jane found herself binge-watching entire seasons of Netflix originals and eagerly awaiting new releases, showcasing how Netflix's adaptive approach to content delivery and recommendation algorithms influenced her viewing habits.

By embracing habit evolution, Netflix has solidified its position as a leader in the streaming industry and continues to shape the future of entertainment. Its commitment to innovation and user-centric design ensures that Netflix remains relevant and indispensable in an ever-changing media landscape.

Netflix's story serves as a compelling example of how businesses can thrive by embracing change and adapting to evolving consumer habits and preferences.[7]

This real-life story of Netflix illustrates how embracing habit evolution can lead to continued success and relevance in a rapidly changing market, showcasing the importance of adaptability and innovation in business strategy.

Practical Tips for Habit Evolution

- **Regular Reflection**: Set aside time for regular reflection on your habits and values, assessing whether they are still aligned.
- **Experimentation**: Be open to trying new habits and approaches, embracing the process of trial and error.
- **Flexibility**: Remain flexible and adaptable, recognizing that habits may need to evolve as your circumstances change.

Conclusion: Embracing the Journey of Habit Evolution

Habit evolution is a natural and essential part of personal growth and development. By embracing the fluidity of habit formation and actively shaping your routines to align with your evolving goals and values, you can ensure that your habits continue to support and enrich your life. Embrace the journey of habit evolution as a pathway to continuous learning, growth, and fulfillment.

In the next chapter, we will explore the concept of habit legacy—how your habits shape not only your own life but also the lives of those around you. Get ready to discover the ripple effects of your habits and the legacy you

---

[7] Reference: Netflix Website and Industry Analysis

leave behind.

CHAPTER 8: THE RIPPLE EFFECTS OF HABIT LEGACY

Introduction: The Impact of Your Habits

Your habits have far-reaching effects that extend beyond your own life. In this chapter, we explore the concept of habit legacy—how your habits shape not only your present but also the future of those around you. By understanding the ripple effects of your habits, you can harness their power to create a positive legacy that influences generations to come.

The Ripple Effect of Habits

Habits create a ripple effect, influencing not only your own life but also the lives of others in your orbit:

- **Personal Impact**: Your habits directly impact your well-being, productivity, and fulfillment.
- **Social Influence**: Your habits influence the behaviors and attitudes of those around you, from family members to colleagues to friends.
- **Generational Legacy**: Your habits can shape the habits and values passed down to future generations, leaving a lasting impact on your family and community.

Modeling Behavior for Others

As a role model, your habits serve as a blueprint for those around you. Strategies for modeling positive habits include:

- **Lead by Example**: Demonstrate the behaviors you wish to see in

others, whether it's healthy living, lifelong learning, or acts of kindness.
- **Share Your Journey**: Be open about your habit journey, sharing successes, challenges, and lessons learned with others.
- **Provide Support**: Offer encouragement and support to those seeking to adopt new habits, serving as a source of inspiration and accountability.

Cultivating a Positive Habit Legacy

To cultivate a positive habit legacy, focus on habits that promote well-being, growth, and connection:

- **Prioritize Self-Care**: Invest in habits that nurture your physical, mental, and emotional health, setting an example for others to follow.
- **Lifelong Learning**: Cultivate habits of curiosity and continuous learning, inspiring others to embrace a growth mindset and pursue their passions.
- **Building Relationships**: Foster habits that strengthen relationships and community ties, creating a sense of belonging and support for those around you.

The Story of Maya: A Legacy of Kindness and Generosity

Maya was known for her acts of kindness and generosity, which left a lasting impact on her community. From volunteering at local shelters to organizing charity events, Maya's habits inspired others to pay it forward and create positive change in the world. Though Maya is no longer with us, her habit legacy lives on in the hearts and actions of those she touched.

Real-Life Example: *Rosa Parks and the Legacy of Courage*

Rosa Parks, often hailed as the "Mother of the Civil Rights Movement," left a profound legacy of courage and activism that continues to inspire generations.

Catalyzing Change:

On December 1, 1955, Rosa Parks made history by refusing to give up her seat to a white passenger on a segregated bus in Montgomery, Alabama. Her act of defiance against unjust segregation laws sparked a wave of protests and boycotts that ultimately led to the desegregation of public transportation in the United States.

Leading by Example:

Rosa Parks's refusal to comply with segregation laws was not a spontaneous act but a deliberate choice rooted in her deeply held beliefs and principles. Throughout her life, Parks had been actively involved in civil rights activism, participating in protests, voter registration drives, and other efforts to combat racial injustice.

Inspiring Others:

Rosa Parks's courageous stand inspired countless individuals to join the fight for civil rights and equality. Her actions galvanized the African American community and brought national attention to the injustices of segregation. Leaders like Martin Luther King Jr. and other civil rights activists rallied behind Parks, turning her act of defiance into a powerful symbol of resistance and solidarity.

Creating Lasting Change:

The ripple effects of Rosa Parks's courage and determination continue to be felt today. Her refusal to accept injustice paved the way for significant advancements in civil rights legislation and social justice movements. Parks's legacy serves as a reminder of the power of individual actions to spark collective change and the importance of standing up for what is right, even in the face of adversity.

An illustrative example is Maya, a young activist who grew up hearing stories of Rosa Parks's bravery and resilience. Inspired by Parks's example, Maya became involved in local activism and advocacy efforts, working to address issues of racial inequality and discrimination in her community. Maya's commitment to social justice and equality is a testament to the enduring impact of Rosa Parks's legacy.

Rosa Parks's story exemplifies how one person's courage and determination can ignite a movement and create lasting change. Her legacy continues to inspire individuals around the world to stand up against injustice and fight for a more equitable society.[8]

---

[8] Reference: Theoharis, J. (2013). The Rebellious Life of Mrs. Rosa Parks. Beacon Press.

This real-life story of Rosa Parks demonstrates how the ripple effects of individual habits of courage and activism can create lasting change and inspire others to join in the pursuit of justice and equality, showcasing the profound impact of personal habits on society as a whole.

Practical Tips for Building a Positive Habit Legacy

- **Lead by Example**: Demonstrate positive habits through your actions and behaviors.
- **Share Your Journey**: Be open about your habit journey, sharing successes and lessons learned with others.
- **Prioritize Well-Being**: Focus on habits that promote health, growth, and connection, leaving a positive legacy for future generations.

Conclusion: Embracing the Power of Habit Legacy

Your habits are more than just routines; they are a reflection of who you are and the impact you leave on the world. By cultivating positive habits and modeling behavior for others, you can create a legacy that inspires and uplifts generations to come. Embrace the power of habit legacy and watch as your influence echoes through time, leaving a lasting imprint on the world.

In the next chapter, we will reflect on the journey of habit transformation and explore strategies for integrating these principles into your daily life. Get ready to embark on a lifelong journey of growth, fulfillment, and positive change.

Chapter 9
Conclusion: The Journey of Habit Transformation

Reflecting on Your Habit Journey
As you reach the end of this book, take a moment to reflect on your habit journey. You've embarked on a transformative adventure, exploring the intricacies of habit formation, from the foundational principles to the ripple effects of habit legacy. Along the way, you've gained insights, strategies, and inspiration to shape your habits and create a life of meaning and fulfillment.

Integrating Habit Principles into Your Life
As you move forward, consider how you can integrate the principles of habit transformation into your daily life:

- **Define Your Identity**: Clarify the person you want to become and align your habits with that vision.
- **Embrace Simplicity**: Streamline your habits for maximum effectiveness and efficiency.
- **Cultivate Satisfaction**: Infuse your habits with meaning, pleasure, and reward to enhance your overall well-being.
- **Maintain Resilience:** Develop resilience and perseverance to overcome challenges and setbacks on your habit journey.
- **Evolve and Adapt**: Embrace the fluidity of habit formation, adapting your habits to align with your evolving goals and values.
- **Create a Positive Legacy**: Harness the power of your habits to

inspire and uplift those around you, leaving a lasting impact on the world.

Real-Life Example: *Tony Robbins and the Power of Personal Development*
Tony Robbins, renowned motivational speaker and life coach, has dedicated his career to helping individuals transform their habits and achieve personal growth and fulfillment.

Starting the Journey:

Tony Robbins's own journey of habit transformation began at a young age when he made a conscious decision to overcome the limitations of his upbringing and strive for success. Through self-reflection, goal-setting, and relentless determination, Robbins embarked on a path of personal development that would shape his life and career.

Developing Empowering Habits:

Robbins attributes much of his success to the development of empowering habits that support his goals and aspirations. He emphasizes the importance of rituals and routines in shaping behavior and mindset, such as daily gratitude practice, visualization exercises, and physical movement. By consistently engaging in these habits, Robbins has cultivated a mindset of abundance, resilience, and growth.

Inspiring Transformation in Others:

Throughout his career, Tony Robbins has inspired millions of people around the world to embark on their own journey of habit transformation. Through his books, seminars, and coaching programs, Robbins shares practical strategies and insights for breaking through limitations, overcoming obstacles, and creating lasting change. His message of personal empowerment and transformation has resonated with individuals from all walks of life, empowering them to take control of their habits and their destinies.

Continuing the Journey:

Despite his immense success, Tony Robbins remains committed to his own journey of habit transformation and personal growth. He continues to refine his habits, explore new challenges, and seek opportunities for learning and development. Robbins's ongoing commitment to growth serves as a powerful reminder that the journey of habit transformation is never truly complete but rather a lifelong process of evolution and discovery.

An illustrative example is Sarah, a participant in one of Tony Robbins's seminars. Sarah had struggled with self-doubt and limiting beliefs for years, holding her back from pursuing her dreams. Through Robbins's guidance and teachings, Sarah was able to identify and reframe her negative thought patterns, develop empowering habits, and take bold action towards her goals. Sarah's transformation is a testament to the profound impact of habit transformation on individual lives.

Tony Robbins's story exemplifies the transformative power of habits and personal development in achieving success, fulfillment, and growth. His journey serves as an inspiration for others to embark on their own path of habit transformation and self-discovery.[9]

This real-life story of Tony Robbins showcases how the journey of habit transformation can lead to profound personal growth and empowerment, inspiring individuals to take control of their habits and create the life they desire.

Embracing the Journey Ahead

Remember that habit transformation is a journey, not a destination. It's about continuous growth, learning, and refinement. Embrace the challenges, celebrate the victories, and stay committed to becoming the best version of yourself.

Your Habit Journey Continues

As you close this chapter, know that your habit journey continues long after you've finished reading. Every action you take, every choice you make, contributes to the ongoing evolution of your habits and your life. Embrace the journey with an open heart and a curious mind, and watch as your habits transform you in ways you never imagined possible.

Thank You

---

[9] Reference: Robbins, T. (1991). Awaken the Giant Within: How to Take Immediate Control of Your Mental, Emotional, Physical and Financial Destiny! Free Press.

Thank you for joining me on this journey of habit transformation. May you continue to cultivate habits that nourish your soul, inspire those around you, and leave a positive legacy for generations to come.

Wishing you continued growth, fulfillment, and success on your habit journey.

With gratitude,
Onome Akiti

Just before you close this book, there is one more thing I want you to see.

The Hidden Pitfalls Of Good Habits

The Story Of Mary: The Perils of Over-Optimization
In the fast-paced world of professional athletics, the pursuit of excellence often comes with the risk of over-optimization and burnout. One such cautionary tale is that of Mary, a competitive long-distance runner who experienced the hidden pitfalls of good habits firsthand.

The Journey to Success:

Mary had always been passionate about running and dedicated herself to rigorous training routines and disciplined habits from a young age. Her commitment and hard work paid off, and she achieved remarkable success in high school and college track competitions. Mary's consistent training and focus on good habits propelled her to the top of her sport, earning her accolades and recognition.

The Downward Spiral:

However, as Mary transitioned to professional competition, the pressure to maintain her success took its toll. Fueled by a desire for perfection and a fear of failure, Mary pushed herself to the limit, often at the expense of her physical and mental well-being. She became obsessed with optimizing every aspect of her training, from diet and sleep to technique and recovery, in pursuit of marginal gains.

The Breaking Point:

Despite her best efforts, Mary began to experience signs of burnout and decline in performance. The relentless pursuit of perfection had left her exhausted, depleted, and disillusioned. Her once-joyful passion for running had turned into a relentless obsession, and she struggled to find meaning and satisfaction in her sport.

The Path to Recovery:

Recognizing the need for change, Mary sought help from coaches, sports psychologists, and fellow athletes who had experienced similar struggles. With their support, Mary gradually shifted her focus from relentless optimization to holistic well-being and balance. She learned to listen to her body, prioritize rest and recovery, and find joy in the process rather than fixating on outcomes.

The Redemption:

Over time, Mary's journey of self-discovery and recovery led to a newfound appreciation for running and a renewed sense of purpose. By embracing a more balanced approach to training and competition, Mary was able to reignite her passion for the sport and achieve success on her own terms. Today, Mary serves as a mentor and advocate for athletes struggling with the hidden pitfalls of over-optimization, sharing her story as a cautionary reminder to prioritize well-being and balance in the pursuit of excellence.

Mary's story serves as a poignant reminder of the hidden dangers that can accompany the relentless pursuit of good habits. While habits are essential for success, it is crucial to maintain perspective, balance, and self-care to avoid falling victim to the pitfalls of over-optimization and burnout.

While the benefits of cultivating good habits are widely recognized, it's equally important to be aware of potential downsides. Understanding these hidden pitfalls can help you navigate the complexities of habit formation and ensure that your habits continue to serve your long-term goals and well-being.

Mary's story illustrates the importance of maintaining balance and perspective when pursuing good habits, highlighting the hidden pitfalls that can arise when striving for perfection at the expense of well-being.

The Illusion of Completion

One common pitfall is the illusion of completion. Once a habit is established, it's easy to fall into the trap of complacency, believing that the work is done. However, maintaining a habit requires ongoing effort and attention. For example, someone who adopts a habit of daily exercise might become complacent after reaching their fitness goals, leading to a gradual decline in their routine and fitness levels.

Story: Jane, a successful entrepreneur, developed a habit of networking by attending industry events every week. Over time, she built a strong network and felt she had achieved her goal. Gradually, she reduced her attendance at these events, and eventually, her network began to weaken as she lost touch with key contacts.

Rigidity and Inflexibility

Good habits can sometimes lead to rigidity and inflexibility. While consistency is key, being too rigid can make it difficult to adapt to new circumstances or changes in your environment. It's important to balance discipline with flexibility, allowing your habits to evolve as needed.

Story: Mark, a dedicated writer, developed a habit of writing for two hours every morning. This routine helped him complete several novels. However, when his family situation changed and he needed to adjust his schedule, Mark struggled to adapt. His rigid adherence to his writing habit caused friction with his family and led to unnecessary stress.

Over-Reliance on Habits

Relying too heavily on habits can stifle creativity and spontaneity. When your day is too structured, there's little room for the unexpected opportunities and experiences that can enrich your life. It's important to strike a balance between routine and spontaneity.

Story: Sarah, a marketing manager, had a meticulously planned daily schedule. Her reliance on routines made her highly efficient, but she began to notice that she was missing out on creative ideas and opportunities for innovation. By making room for unstructured time, Sarah was able to rekindle her creativity and bring fresh ideas to her work.

Habit Stacking Gone Wrong

Habit stacking, or linking new habits to established ones, is a powerful technique. However, if not done carefully, it can lead to overwhelming and unsustainable routines. Adding too many new habits at once can result in burnout and a complete abandonment of your efforts.

Story: Alex, an ambitious student, tried to stack multiple new habits onto his existing routine: exercising, learning a new language, and reading for an hour each day. Initially, he managed to keep up, but soon found himself exhausted and overwhelmed. Unable to sustain the demanding routine, Alex ended up abandoning all his new habits.

The Pressure of Perfection

The pursuit of perfection can be a significant downside of good habits. Striving for an unbroken streak or flawless execution can create immense pressure and anxiety. This perfectionism can be detrimental to your mental health and can lead to discouragement if you inevitably miss a day or fall short of your high standards.

Story: Emily, a dedicated meditator, prided herself on her 365-day meditation streak. One busy day, she missed her session and felt devastated. This single lapse made her question her commitment and led to a temporary abandonment of her practice. Overcoming the need for perfection, Emily learned to focus on the long-term benefits rather than daily perfection.

Recognizing and Mitigating Pitfalls

To avoid these pitfalls, it's essential to remain mindful of the broader context and purpose of your habits. Regularly reassess your routines to ensure they align with your goals and values. Incorporate flexibility into your habits and be gentle with yourself when you face setbacks.

Tips to Mitigate Pitfalls:

- **Regular Reflection**: Periodically review your habits to ensure they continue to serve your goals and well-being.
- **Adaptability**: Be willing to adjust your habits in response to changes in your life or environment.
- **Balance**: Strike a balance between routine and spontaneity to foster creativity and avoid rigidity.
- **Moderation**: Avoid overloading yourself with too many new habits at once; prioritize sustainability.

- **Self-Compassion**: Practice self-compassion and avoid the trap of perfectionism. Embrace progress over perfection.

By being aware of these hidden pitfalls and taking proactive steps to mitigate them, you can cultivate good habits that are sustainable, flexible, and truly beneficial in the long run.

ABOUT THE AUTHOR

Onome Akiti is a seasoned IT Expert and Life Coach with a wealth of experience in training both young and older minds in the ever-evolving landscape of the 21st century. With a passion for steady growth, change management, and personal development, Onome has dedicated his career to helping individuals and organizations navigate the complexities of the digital age.

Throughout his career, Onome has been driven by a deep-seated belief in the transformative power of small steps. Recognizing that meaningful change often begins with incremental progress, he has made it his mission to empower others to embrace the journey of continuous improvement and self-discovery.

An avid enthusiast of futuristic technologies, Onome is constantly exploring emerging trends and innovations that have the potential to shape the future. From artificial intelligence to virtual reality, he is fascinated by anything that strengthens the mind and expands the boundaries of human potential.

In addition to his professional pursuits, Onome is a devoted husband to his wife, Damilola, and a proud father to their daughter, Nicole. His commitment to family serves as a constant source of inspiration and motivation in his quest to help others become the best version of themselves.

As the author of "The Power of Small Steps," Onome brings together his expertise in IT, his passion for personal growth, and his dedication to empowering others to create a roadmap for transformational change. Through this book, he shares his insights, strategies, and wisdom to guide readers on a journey of self-discovery, growth, and fulfillment.

With Onome Akiti as your guide, you'll discover the power of small steps to unlock your full potential and embark on a path toward becoming the best version of yourself.